Practicing Extravagant Generosity

Practicing
Extravagant
GENEROSITY

Daily Readings on the Grace of Giving

ROBERT SCHNASE

ABINGDON PRESS
Nashville, Tennessee

PRACTICING EXTRAVAGANT GENEROSITY:
DAILY READINGS ON THE GRACE OF GIVING

This book is printed on acid-free paper.

Library of Congress Cataloging-in-Publication Data

Schnase, Robert
  Practicing extravagant generosity : daily readings on the grace of
giving / Robert Schnase.
    p. cm.
  ISBN 978-1-4267-2855-6 (pbk. : alk. paper)
  1. Christian giving--Prayers and devotions. 2. United Methodist
Church (U.S.)--Prayers and devotions. 3. Christian giving--United
Methodist Church (U.S.) I. Title.
  BV772.S343 2011
  248'.6--dc22
                                    2010051745

**The daily readings found in this book are adapted from the previous writings of the
author, including *Five Practices of Fruitful Congregations*, *Five Practices of Fruitful
Living*, *Cultivating Fruitfulness: Five Weeks of Prayer and Practice for Congregations*, *The
Balancing Act: A Daily Rediscovery of Grace*, and from blogs by Robert Schnase published
at FivePractices.org.**

17 18 19 20 - 15 16 17 18
MANUFACTURED IN THE UNITED STATES OF AMERICA

CONTENTS

WELCOME

Giving helps us become what God wants us to be. Giving is not merely about the church's need for money but about the Christian's need to grow in generosity. Generosity is a fruit of the Spirit, a sign of our spiritual growth. God uses our giving to change the world for God's purposes, and God uses our giving to reconfigure our interior lives and to change us!

Over the next four weeks, you're invited to join in brief daily readings with everyone else in your congregation.* Each reading prepares you; your pastor; and all congregational leaders, members, and guests to understand more clearly the "why" of Christian giving and to develop a common language and theology of generosity. Everyone praying, reading, and reflecting on the same passages fosters a unified sense of purpose and clarity of mission. Your participation with an open heart helps open the doors of your church's future mission. Thank you!

Each reading includes a Scripture verse and a brief devotion. Read thoughtfully, reflecting on your own faith journey and your congregation's ministry. Use the questions to prompt further spiritual exploration about what you think, believe, and do. Close your time with prayer. Feel free to discuss your reflections with others in your household or from the congregation who are reading the same stories for the day, or make note of your thoughts in the journaling space provided at the end of each week.

I pray these weeks may be for you a time of spiritual growth and renewed commitment to the ministry of Christ through your congregation.

Yours in Christ,

Robert Schnase

* *Practicing Extravagant Generosity: Daily Readings on the Grace of Giving* has been prepared for use with the congregation-wide stewardship program *Extravagant Generosity: The Heart of Giving* by Michael Reeves and Jennifer Tyler (Abingdon Press, 2011; UPC 843504019143). While these readings may be used with other stewardship programs, the themes align particularly with topics, strategies, timelines, and media materials of the Extravagant Generosity model.

Week One

FROM STEWARDSHIP TO GENEROSITY

"Giving, not getting, is the way.
Generosity begets generosity."
— *Luke 6:38,* **The Message**

A few years ago, I had the privilege of speaking at a training seminar at a large United Methodist church. My host was on staff at the church, and he described how he had recently changed his title after reflecting upon the *Five Practices of Fruitful Congregations*. Formerly the Executive Director of Stewardship, he was now the Executive Director of *Generosity*. He, the other staff, and the congregational leaders decided "generosity" comes closer than "stewardship" to describing his purpose and role.

This made me think. What's the difference between "stewardship" and "generosity"? What comes to mind when you hear those words? For what distinctive purposes are they best suited? How do people respond to those terms?

We are stewards of the earth. We are stewards of those things entrusted to us, inherited by us, and earned by us. We are stewards of our wealth and possessions and physical bodies. Stewards are people in ancient times who were trustees, who had responsibilities, who cared for things owned by someone else. Today you don't hear much about stewards and steward-ship outside the church; it's a language derived from our bib-lical roots and our church heritage. It risks becoming insider language, not easily accessible or immediately understandable by those new to the church. There is something slightly weighty, dutiful, and legal sounding about the word. I grew up hearing about stewardship, stewardship campaigns, and com-mittees on stewardship. The language focused our attention on supporting the church financially.

Generosity is an aspect of character. It is an attractive quality which I aspire to and desire to see cultivated in my children. The opposite of generosity is selfishness, self-cen-teredness, greed, and self-absorption. No stories from Scrip-ture tell of people living the God-related spiritual life while fostering a greedy attitude. Generosity extends beyond merely the use of money, although it most definitely includes that. There are generous spirits; generous souls; people who are generous with their time, with their teaching, with their love. Generosity finds many biblical sources, and is a fruit of the Spirit (Galatians 5:22-23). It sounds more organic, more gen-erative, less legalistic, less formal than stewardship. I have to explain to my teenage sons what stewardship means. They know generosity when they see it.

I admire and respect people who are generous, and I want to become like them. Generosity is not a spiritual attribute someone acquires apart from the actual practice of giving. It becomes discernable through action. We never describe people as generous who keep everything for themselves and only serve themselves.

Generosity focuses on the spiritual qualities of the giver, derived from the generosity of God, rather than on the church's need for money. One of these terms is not superior to the other. Perhaps there are shades of differences in how they are perceived by young and old, those new to the faith from those long-established in our churches. Using both wisely helps us reach people at different places on the journey of faith.

- What has been your experience with the term "stewardship"? With "generosity"? What's the difference between them?
- Which most helpfully inspires your giving as you seek to grow in the image of God and in service to Christ?

BUILDING NESTS

*"And the things you have prepared,
whose will they be?"*
— Luke 12:20

One March morning, I saw a large Red-Tailed Hawk fly overhead carrying a long heavy stick. I smiled at this indisputable sign of spring. Non-migratory birds of my area were beginning to build nests. Earlier I had seen an American Crow carrying straw for the same purpose, and the day before I had watched House Sparrows tucking threads of grass into the hole in a convenience store awning.

During the months to come, birds of all kinds would pour extraordinary effort, time, and ingenuity to the construction of nests, the protection of eggs, and the feeding of their vulnerable young ones. After the little ones hatch, I'm always amazed at the unceasing care offered by the parents. Every ounce of the adults' energy is devoted, not to their own comfort and feeding, but to the survival of their young.

The notion of building nests is often used as a metaphor to describe people successfully providing for their own comforts.

If someone arrives at a career position of some ease and security, friends say, "You've built yourself quite a nest for yourself here!" When we are comfortable, secure, and feel at home in our workplace or living area, we talk about the space being "our own little nest." The word *nest* often connotes shelter, coziness, homelike, comfortable.

In actual fact, the nests which birds build are not for the birds who build them, but for their young, for the next generation, for the future of the species. The hours of carrying straw, sticks, and mud; the days of defensive watchfulness; and the weeks of endless feeding are all for the benefit of the new ones, the young, the future.

Now consider "nests" we build in our churches. The buildings, programs, ministries, job descriptions, and services we build—are they for our own comfort and coziness? Or are they to further the faith and provide for future generations? Does our giving serve us and our needs or serve God by serving the mission of the church to reach new people? Vibrant, fruitful congregations focus as much energy, prayer, and planning on those who are outside the congregation as they do on those who are already active in the congregation. When they initiate new Bible studies, outreach ministries, or worship services, they give less emphasis to "what do I want, prefer, or find convenient" and place more weight on "what will feed the souls, nourish the spirits, and sustain the steps" of those outside the church or new to the faith. Those new to the faith are as vulnerable as hatchlings, and require a steady and dedicated effort of feeding. And the budding faith of young people requires our committed attention; extra care; overtime in planning, teaching, encouraging, generosity, mentoring, and support. For those who practice Extravagant Generosity, the nests we build are not for ourselves—they are for the next generation, those new to the faith, the future of the body of Christ.

- What motivates you to support the ministries of your congregation?
- How does your focus on generosity and level of giving support the mission of reaching other people with the grace of God you have received?

SEEDS WITH WINGS

"A sower went out to sow his seed . . ."
— Luke 8:5

As I was hiking with my sons one morning, we noticed a number of large trees dispersing their seeds in a most fascinating way. The seeds were pea-sized with a single leaf-like extension about the size and shape of a large dragonfly wing. Under the weight of the seedpod, the single angled wing would cause the seed to fall with the perfect twirling, rotating motion of a helicopter. The effect was like the "paper helicopters" some of us used to make in elementary school. The seeds whirled around us, slowly descending from the tall trees, and often getting caught up in the breeze to be carried far from the parent tree. It was a delightful sight.

Jesus tells about a sower who goes out to sow, scattering seeds left and right, near and far. Some of the seeds fall on rocky paths, some are scooped up by hungry birds, and some are choked by weeds. But some find fertile soil, take root, and a harvest comes forth beyond what any of us can imagine. He tells the parable to remind us of the way our faithful efforts make a difference in the lives of others around us.

Watching the "seeds with wings," as my son called them, added a new dimension to Jesus' parable of the seeds and soils. So much of our impact, even when we live immensely fruitful lives, affects those closest to us. We are like trees whose seeds fall directly to the ground beneath their own branches and under their own shade. We naturally have the greatest impact upon those closest at hand, our families, spouses, children, and grandchildren. We bear much fruit this way, but in a narrow and limited field. The branches of trees that drop their seeds directly beneath them protect their seedlings, filter sunlight for their good, and provide fallen leaves to nurture them. Among the most important seeds we sow are the grace and love of God we offer within our own families and among our own kindred. This is our calling.

Each of us has another and larger calling as well, and that is to give our seeds wings so that the good we do and the difference we make extend beyond our sight and beyond our time.

Each of us has been formed by the influences of countless people—friends, coworkers, mentors, teachers, coaches, neighbors, pastors, youth sponsors, scout leaders, colleagues, confidants—who have contributed far beyond their own small circles. Through their generosity, time, effort, and love, they have changed us, and changed the world, by intentionally providing a legacy that extends far and wide.

I'm often amazed at the immeasurable difference people make with their lives far away from their homes and long after their deaths. In Honduras, I'll see a clinic started by a Sunday school class from a church in Oklahoma many years ago. In an African village, I'll see kids nestled under mosquito nets funded by youth from a church in Germany. In an American church, I see prayer cloths handmade by Christians in Korea.

In nursing homes, I see birthday cards made by five year olds, and in church nurseries I find blankets knitted by the elderly homebound.

There is no end to what God can accomplish anywhere in the world when our "seeds have wings"; when we are willing to let our prayers, intentions, plans, efforts, and work be lifted by the Spirit to places far away; when our generosity moves beyond ourselves.

- Think of two or three of the most influential people in forming your own soul and character other than your relatives. What made them effective? What can you learn from their generosity and the legacy they have left for others?
- Where in the world beyond your own church and home are there signs of your congregation's ministry? Of your own?

PARTNERING WITH GOD

"They are to do good, to be rich in good works, generous, and ready to share, thus storing up for themselves the treasure of a good foundation for the future, so that they may take hold of the life that really is life."
— 1 Timothy 6:18-19

Paul and Carolyn have been leaders in their congregation for years, and their generosity has grown steadily as they have matured in faith. They also have enjoyed personal financial success. When their church felt called to reach more people and younger generations by building a new sanctuary, Paul and Carolyn were challenged to give a major gift. They prayed about it for weeks, before deciding to give the largest gift they had ever given in their lives. "I felt like I was asked to partner with God for a great purpose," Paul said. "Our gift became one of the great delights of our lives. We loved knowing that we could make a difference. We were deeply moved by the experience." Carolyn adds, "If God gives you the capacity and the passion to do something, why in God's name wouldn't you do it?"

People give because generosity helps them achieve God's purposes in *themselves*. By giving, we develop the inner qualities of generosity. Generosity is not a spiritual attribute someone acquires apart from the practice of giving. It becomes discernable only through visible behavior. We cannot become generous and cling to everything we have without letting go. The opposite of generosity is greediness, selfishness. These are not the qualities that lead to life, and so by our giving we cultivate a different nature inside ourselves.

God uses our practice of giving to reconfigure our interior life. By giving, we craft a different inner desire as the driving element of life. Our motivations change.

Giving moderates the powerful and sometimes destructively insatiable drive for acquisition. In the daily interior struggle fostered by a consumerist, materialist society that pressures us to pursue many things that do not lead to real happiness, the practice of giving aims us at what ultimately satisfies. Giving sanctifies and deepens the struggle, and constantly resets the internal compass in the right direction. Generosity becomes a tool God uses to draw us closer to God and to align us more closely with God's desire for us.

- Have you ever given over and beyond your normal tithe or pattern of giving? If so, what was the experience like?
- Do you find that the more you give, the more likely you are to give? Why or why not?

21

MUSCLE MEMORY

*"Therefore, show . . . the proof of your love
and the reason for our pride in you, so that
the churches can see it."*
— 2 Corinthians 8:24, NIV

Sarah grew up in a family that practiced tithing, and as a child she put ten cents in the offering plate from each dollar she received. She remembers receiving her first paycheck of $56 from her first job as a teenager, and her sense of achievement and delight when she gave $5.60 to the church. Now in her forties, Sarah has a high-paying job as a senior executive, and tithing continues to feel natural, a regular pattern of her life. She does it with ease and grace. "I love giving," she says, "and I cannot imagine living my life or loving God without giving back. Giving is one of the great joys of my life. Tithing was learned and practiced so early that I developed the muscle memory for giving. Like practicing my tennis serve for so many years that I don't have to think about each step, my giving is part of who I am." For someone beginning to tithe, Sarah's level of discipleship may appear unachievable. But with practice, anyone can develop spiritual "muscle memory."

As those who consistently practice the tithe know, proportional giving (giving a set percentage of income) and tithing force people to look at their earning, saving, and spending through God's eyes. It reminds them that their ultimate worth is derived from the assurance that they are children of God, created by God, and infinitely loved by God. God's eternal love revealed in Christ is the source of self-worth; true happiness and meaning are found in growing in grace and in the knowledge and love of God.

Giving generously reprioritizes lives and helps people distinguish what is lasting, eternal, and of infinite value from what is temporary, illusory, and untrustworthy. The discipline of generous giving places people on the balcony, helping them look out at the consumerist society with new perspective, better able to see its traps, deceptions, and myths. The practice of generosity is a means by which God builds people up, strengthens their spirits, and equips them to serve God's purposes.

- Read 2 Corinthians 8. Paul concludes by saying that our giving is a proof of our love for God. Can we possibly desire God to shape our souls without giving?
- If you practice proportional giving or tithing, does this practice affect your other spending habits?
- If you do not practice proportional giving or tithing, what are the obstacles to a greater generosity toward God?

POCKET CHANGE

"The fruit of the Spirit is love, joy, peace, patience,
kindness, generosity, faithfulness, gentleness,
and self-control."
— Galatians 5:22-23

A woman from a small congregation told me about how she led discussions about the book *Five Practices of Fruitful Congregations* in her home with a dozen folks. On the first night, she placed a large Tupperware bowl on a table. As the group finished the discussion, she asked everyone to empty his or her pockets, purses, and wallets of change . . . not bills, just coins. Everyone played along, trying to guess what she was up to. She repeated this mysterious request each week as they studied the book together. Each week, more and more money filled the bowl.

On the last night as they talked about Extravagant Generosity, she revealed her plan. She intended to donate the money to the Nothing But Nets campaign, the extraordinary effort to save lives in Africa by providing medicated mosquito nets to prevent people from getting malaria (www.NothingButNets.net/). They had accumulated over $300 in change—enough to buy thirty nets! This painless and enjoyable exercise while studying the book will save children's lives on the other side of the world. Even pocket change changes lives. Change the life of a child and you change the world.

Generosity is a fruit of the Spirit, a worthy spiritual aspiration. To practice Extravagant Generosity requires self-control, patience, kindness, faith, and love of God and neighbor. These build us up; equip us for life and for ministry; and foster perspectives and attitudes that are sustaining, enriching, and meaningful. Giving changes the giver, the recipient, and the congregation.

This small congregation is learning discipleship, deepening their own faith through study together, practicing simple generosity, and changing the lives of people they will never know while they are also allowing God to change them and their church.

- How does your church change lives in your community? On the other side of the world?
- What will you do to change someone's life this week?

THE GRACE OF GIVING

"But just as you excel in everything—in faith, in speech, in knowledge, in complete earnestness and in your love for us—see that you also excel in this grace of giving."
— 2 Corinthians 8:7, NIV

Churches that practice Extravagant Generosity don't talk in general terms about stewardship; they speak confidently and faithfully about money, giving, generosity, and the difference giving makes for the purposes of Christ and in the life of the giver. They emphasize the Christian's need to give more than the church's need for money. They teach, preach, and practice proportional giving with the goal of tithing. They use God's name accurately by appealing to the highest of life-giving purposes for giving rather than employing fear, guilt, pressure, and shame as motivation.

Churches that cultivate giving speak of joy, devotion, honoring God, and the steady growth of spirit that leads to greater generosity. They don't apologize, whine, groan, act embarrassed, or feel awkward as they encourage people to offer their best to God. People delight in giving. Pledge campaigns are not about money, dollars, and budgets but about mission, spiritual growth, and relationship to God. Stewardship efforts deepen prayer life, build community, unite people with purpose, and clarify mission. People feel strengthened and grateful to serve God through giving.

Churches that practice Extravagant Generosity encourage people to grow in their giving, to give more now than in the past and more in the future than they do today. They share honest stories of lives changed by practicing generosity; they invite people to bear witness to how giving affects their spiritual lives. They publicly thank God for the generosity of the people, and they express personal appreciation time and time again to those who give. They cultivate the hearts of their people in the way of Christ.

Extravagantly generous congregations emphasize mission, purpose, and life-changing results rather than shortages, budgets, and institutional loyalty. They provide a compelling vision that invites people to give joyously, thereby finding purpose, meaning, and satisfaction in changing lives. They know that God moves people to give in order to find purpose and to accomplish things for Christ. They connect money with mission. They give offerings of whatever they can, whenever they can—they excel in the grace of giving, as Paul says (2 Corinthians 8:7).

- How do you feel about how your congregation teaches about money?
- What conversations that relate faith and money are most helpful to you?

Week One Reflections

WEEK TWO

AS IF FOR THE VERY FIRST TIME

". . . I do want you to experience the blessing that issues from generosity."
— Philippians 4:15, The Message

The practice of *generosity* describes the Christian's unselfish willingness to give in order to make a positive difference for the purposes of Christ. *Extravagant Generosity* describes practices of sharing and giving that exceed all expectations and extend to unexpected measures. It describes lavish sharing, sacrifice, and giving in service to God and neighbor.

Charles Frazier, in his novel of the American Civil War, *Cold Mountain*, introduces a minor character, a fiddler whose life is changed through an incident that causes him to look at his musical talents in a whole new way.

The fiddler is a drunk, who knows only six songs. His military unit camps near a house where there's a powerful explosion. A young girl is severely burned and is near death, and her father sends for a fiddler to help ease her way to heaven. The fiddler enters the dark cabin where the young girl suffers in excruciating pain. From her deathbed, she says, "Play me something." He plays a tune. "Play me another." The fiddler plays his drinking tunes slowly, thinking it more appropriate to the circumstances. Soon he has exhausted his small repertoire. "Play me another," she says as she struggles against the pain. "Don't know no more," he says. "That's pitiful," she says, "what kind of a fiddler are you? Make me up a tune then." He marvels at such a strange request. But he has a go at it. Soon the girl passes away. Her father thanks the fiddler for lifting her to heaven with his fiddle.

A transformation takes place, and the author writes, "Time and time again during the walk back to camp the fiddler stopped and looked at his fiddle as if for the very first time. He had never before thought of trying to improve his playing, but now it seemed worthwhile to go at every tune. . . ."[1] Thereafter, he never tired of trying to improve his playing, and he went into taverns of every kind to study the sounds and methods of other musicians. "From that day . . . on, music came more and more into his mind. . . . His playing was as easy as a man drawing breath, yet with utter conviction in its centrality to a life worth claiming."[2]

Imagine the difference he made in the lives of people and the meaning that was added to his own life. That ordinary fiddle and the simple gift of music, when used for higher purposes, became sacred. When the fiddler discovered the gift he had been given, and the power of that gift to influence the world for good, he was changed. His ordinary talent became beautiful, a source of joy and meaning.

We find something similar through the practice of Extravagant Generosity. Giving causes life. Before, our giving may have been arbitrary, perfunctory, haphazard, a little here and there. But when we discover the great difference generosity makes; place it in service to God; and use our resources to relieve suffering, strengthen communities, and restore relationships, then we look at giving entirely differently. We look at our giving, and see it as if for the very first time. We want to improve on our generosity at every turn until it becomes as easy as drawing breath.

Through our generosity, God can do extraordinary things. Through our giving, God changes lives, and in changing them, transforms us.

- When was a time you felt God transformed your life because you gave?
- What ways will you improve your generosity?

WHITEWATER WORLD!

*"Keep your eyes on Jesus, who both began and
finished this race we're in. Study how he did it.
Because he never lost sight of where he was
headed—that exhilarating finish in and with God—
he could put up with anything along the way . . ."*
— *Hebrews 12:2,* The Message

Ever wonder why rafters and canoeists paddle while going
downstream?

I've spent much time canoeing and kayaking over the
years, but I learned about currents, rapids, and whitewater in
Central America. While studying Spanish in Costa Rica, my
sons and I took a weekend break and joined a raft trip on the
Pacuare River. The rapids were posted as Level Three, but the
river was swollen, and the ratings didn't match U.S. measure-
ments. Once we got on the water it felt like we were heading
over Niagara Falls, over and over again, hour after hour, fre-
quently finding ourselves flung out of the raft and struggling
for our lives in the deep and dangerous currents. I don't wish
to repeat the experience anytime soon. The T-shirt my boys
bought afterward read, *"Remar o Morir!"* Paddle or Die!

The guide sat at the back of the raft calling out instructions
about which side to paddle on, and how intensely to do so.

During a period of relative calm, as the river was propelling us down toward the next deathtrap, the guide told us to paddle gently but steadily. My son asked, "Why do we have to paddle when the river is pushing us downstream anyway?" He smiled and said, "The only way we have any control over the direction we are going is for us to be moving just a little faster than the current below us. So we have to paddle constantly, or else we just get pushed along out of control." If we want to navigate with purpose and to control our direction rather than becoming a victim to forces beyond our control, we have to keep paddling. "Remar o Morir!"

We live in a whitewater world. Things change so rapidly—communications systems, the makeup of our communities, the tastes and habits of new generations, the expectations and values of congregations, the competing claims of a secular society for our hearts and minds. This is true in our personal and family lives as well—the phases and steps of a marriage, the transitions of our children, the heartbreaks and hopes, deaths and births, losses and gains, brokenness and reconciliation. Unceasing motion. We live fast-forward lives.

Life pushes us along, and sometimes there seems little we can do; we feel like victims, vulnerable and powerless. But we can't stop paddling. We can't stop learning, growing, changing, adapting, and giving our best. It's by rethinking things, praying anew each day, and by constantly recommitting to the right things that we embrace God's will for us so that we are able to navigate through the whitewater world. It's by depending upon friends, knowing the water, and repeatedly practicing the disciplines that keep us connected to God that we remain strong.

Life requires an agility of spirit, forward movement, effort, vision, and a keen awareness of the forces at work around us and how to use them for the purposes of Christ rather than become overwhelmed by them.

Keep paddling!

- What are the pressures and currents of your whitewater world?
- How do you learn, adapt, grow, and change spiritually so the currents don't overwhelm and destroy you?

WHAT HAPPENS TO GOD'S LOVE?

*"If you see some brother or sister in need and have
the means to do something about it but turn a cold
shoulder and do nothing, what happens to God's
love? It disappears. And you made it disappear. My
dear children, let's not just talk about love; let's
practice real love. This is the only way we'll know
we're living truly, living in God's reality."*
— *1 John 3:17-19*, The Message

A downtown congregation in a moderately-sized community had occasional homeless persons who would ask for hand-
outs. Sometimes street people would be found sleeping on the
front steps. The staff developed rules, guidelines, and policies
for how to help or where to refer those who asked for help.
They had many discussions about the pros and cons of giving
cash, vouchers, and addresses of other social agencies.

As the pastor was leaving the church one afternoon, he
noticed the part-time custodian carrying out the garbage to the
large trash bin in the alley. There was a homeless person
sprawled out beside the bin, barely conscious. As the custodian approached the trash bin, he set down the garbage bag he
was carrying, pulled out his wallet, and removed a few dollar

bills. Without being asked, he walked over to the homeless man and gave him the money, said something, then continued his work and returned to the church. The pastor was amazed and humbled by this extraordinary display of generosity. The part-time janitor who earned less than anyone else on staff gave generously without even being asked, while the staff had spent hours trying to figure out policies and procedures.

The pastor asked the custodian why he gave the money and pressed him about whether he thought the homeless person might misuse the money for alcohol or drugs. "I always do what I can," the janitor answered. "I give them a little money and say, God bless you, because I figure that they are some mother's son, some father's child, and so I give them something. What they do with the money—well, they have to answer to God about that. I have to answer to God about what I do with mine."

- Have you ever witnessed an extraordinary and unexpected act of generosity?
- How has another person's generosity influenced your own practice of giving?
- Who is learning from your examples of generosity?

OWNERSHIP

*"Every good and perfect gift is from above, coming
down from the Father of the heavenly lights."*
— James 1:17, NIV

Fundamentally, we either consider the material things in
our life—our money, house, property—as owned by God and
belonging to God, and we manage them for God's purposes, or
we view them as owned by us. If they are owned by God, then
our tithes and offerings represent our returning to God what
belongs to God already. What we keep also belongs to God,
and we feel obligated to spend it wisely and not frivolously,
and to invest it in ways that do not dishonor God's purposes.
We try not to waste money or to live more lavishly than we
should. We spend responsibly, allowing our relationship with
God to form our minds. We manage God's resources as faithfully as we can.

But if we believe that our material resources fundamentally belong to us and that we entirely possess them ourselves,
then we can do whatever we please with what we own, and our
tithes and offerings are giving something that belongs to us, to
God. God should be grateful for our generosity in giving a percentage for God's purposes rather than our feeling grateful for
the privilege of using what belongs to God.

Think about the possession of land. Suppose we hold legal title and own land according to civil authorities. In the larger span of the earth's history, does our patch of soil actually belong to us, or are we temporary stewards? The land didn't begin with us and doesn't end with us. The land we claim to own has existed for millions of years, was used by humans for millennia before us, and will remain for eons more after we are gone. For the ordering of civil life, we rightly say we own the property and it belongs to us. But our mortality assures that we are only the temporary stewards, managers, and keepers. At our dying, what will the things we own mean to us? Whose will they be? People live and perish, but purposes are eternal. With that understanding comes a profound and humble sense of responsibility about how we use the land. It's temporarily ours to enjoy, but we do so with respect and awe, because ultimately everything belongs to God, and not to us.

This concrete example applies to all of the temporal elements of our lives—our possessions, our wealth, even our bodies and minds. Which perspective is truer, more ethically sound, more aligned with reality? That it all belongs to us and we can do whatever we want? Or that we are the temporary beneficiaries, and we find meaning in using what God has entrusted to us to the highest purposes? Which perspective fosters better decisions and deepens a spiritually grounded sense of community and responsibility? The wisdom revealed in Scripture and tradition for more than three thousand years is that those who practice from the perspective of a steward find greater happiness.

- Which of these two views do you hold?
- How does this belief shape your actions? Your giving?

Friday

ROBUST MINISTRIES

"But seek first his kingdom and his righteousness,
and all these things will be given to you as well."
— Matthew 6:33, NIV

It is through giving of ourselves as God has given to us
that we help the body of Christ flourish. Offering our material
resources to God is a fundamental activity that is so critical to
the church's mission that failure to perform it in an exemplary
way leads to the decline of the church. Churches that nurture
proportional giving and tithing among their members thrive.
They accomplish great things for Christ, offer robust and con-
fident ministry, and they prosper for the purposes of Christ and
make a difference in the lives of people.

Every sanctuary and chapel in which we have worshiped,
every church organ that has lifted our spirits, every pew where
we have sat, every Communion rail where we have knelt, every
hymnal from which we have sung, every praise band that has
touched our hearts, every church classroom where we have
gathered with our friends, every church kitchen that has prepared our meals, every church van that has taken us to camp,
every church camp cabin where we have slept—all are the fruit
of someone's Extravagant Generosity.

We have been the recipients of grace upon grace. We are the heirs, the beneficiaries of those who came before us who were touched by the generosity of Christ enough to give graciously so that we could experience the truth of Christ for ourselves. We owe the same to generations to come. We have worshiped in sanctuaries that we did not build, so to us falls the privilege of building sanctuaries where we shall never worship.

People who practice Extravagant Generosity pray for their congregations to flourish in the ministry of Christ for children, youth, adults, members, and strangers near and far. They serve the church, offering their best efforts. They push the church to offer bold and vital ministries that transform the world, relieving suffering, deepening justice, encouraging love. And they give—regularly, generously, sacrificially, faithfully, and humbly.

Extravagant Generosity is not just about the church's need to receive, but about the Christian's need to give. Generosity is an essential quality of spiritual maturity and growth. The practice of Extravagant Generosity changes churches.

- How have you been the recipient of another person's Extravagant Generosity?
- Have you been the recipient of a congregation's Extravagant Generosity? Of God's?

Saturday

ALL THE GOOD YOU CAN

*"You are familiar with the generosity of our Master,
Jesus Christ. Rich as he was, he gave it all away for
us—in one stroke he became poor and we became
rich." — 2 Corinthians 8:9,* **The Message**

Where God's Spirit is present, people give. John Wesley, the founder of Methodism, wrote:

Do all the good you can,
By all the means you can,
In all the ways you can,
In all the places you can,
At all the times you can,
To all the people you can,
As long as ever you can.

John Wesley taught extensively about the use of money, the danger of riches, and the importance of giving. For Wesley, all things belong to God. This changes how we perceive the manner by which we *earn* money and *save* money, causing us to do so in appropriate ways. And it changes how we *spend* money, making us more responsible, and shapes how we *give* money. Wesley valued industrious and productive

43

work, but he believed that acquiring money does not provide a profound enough life purpose to sustain the human spirit. When he wrote, "Earn all you can, save all you can, and give all you can," he drew an unbreakable link between acquisition and generosity, inviting us to use our material wealth to deepen our relationship with God and to increase our positive impact for God's purposes.

No stories from Scripture tell of people living the God-related spiritual life while fostering a greedy, self-centered, self-serving attitude. Knowing God leads to generosity.

- How does generosity and giving change the values that guide your earning, saving, and spending habits?
- How does your relationship to God affect how you earn your money? How you invest it? How you spend it? Have you ever changed how you earn, invest, or spend because of your desire to follow Christ more truly?

FIRST THINGS FIRST

*"But seek first his kingdom and his righteousness,
and all these things will be given to you as well."*
— Matthew 6:33, NIV

When asked how much money they would need to earn to be happy, people of all different incomes answer the same. If they could only earn about twenty percent more than they presently do, they would finally arrive at a satisfying happiness. Persons earning $10,000 dream of reaching $12,000; those earning $100,000 believe that with just $20,000 more per year they will be happy; and people earning $500,000 believe that when they earn $100,000 more they will finally arrive. We pursue a receding goal. This is a prescription for never-ending unhappiness. We can never possess enough to satiate the appetite for more. Single-minded pursuit of lifestyles highlighted by pop culture keeps us stuck on the surface of existence, captured in the material world, unhappy with what we possess, and blind to the real riches.

When we accept unreflectively the myths of money, we suffer from a self-created, culturally-fostered discontent.

Forty-year-olds feel like failures because they are not millionaires; families buy houses beyond their capacity to afford; people pine for what they cannot possess. We wallow in abundance while suffering from a self-proclaimed scarcity. Despite the fact that we live in better houses, earn more money, drive nicer cars, spend more on entertainment, and enjoy greater conveniences than ninety percent of the world's population, or than we ourselves enjoyed thirty years ago, we never have enough.

We are surrounded by inducements that make us acutely and painfully aware of what we lack, more so than of what we have. Without beliefs and intentional practices that counterbalance the influences of culture, we feel discontent no matter how much we have.

Extravagant giving is a means of putting God first, a method for declaring to God and to ourselves the rightful order of priorities. When we practice it, we live with a more relaxed posture about money, less panicked and reactive. We take possession instead of being possessed. Money becomes a servant rather than our master. By provoking us to give, God is not trying to take something from us; God is seeking to give something to us. Every time we spend money, we make a statement about what we value. All inducements to spend money (advertising, social expectation, seeking to impress people) are attempts to shape our values. When we fail to conscientiously decide what we value and align our spending habits accordingly, a thousand other inducements and voices stand ready to define our values instead. Giving provides a spiritually healthy detachment from the most harmful influences of a materialist society, an emotional distance that is otherwise unattainable. Giving protects us from the pangs of greed.

The practice of generosity opens us to deeper reflection and conversation about wealth and how it relates to purpose and happiness. Serious giving leads us to ask, What is our family's definition of success? How wealthy do we hope we, or our children, will be, and why? What motivates us as a household, and what matters most to our happiness? What will become of the wealth we accumulate?

How much do we give, and why? What difference do we want to make in the world? How does giving influence our relationship with God? What does Extravagant Generosity mean for us? For God? These and other questions can only be asked with authenticity when they are supported by the practice of giving. Giving fosters intentionality.

- How does your family talk about money and what makes for true happiness?
- How wealthy do you hope your children become, and why?

Week Two Reflections

WEEK THREE

Monday

THE JOY OF GIVING

"How can I repay the LORD
for all his goodness to me?"
— Psalm 116:12, NIV

Scripture is replete with examples and teachings that focus on possessions, wealth, giving, gifts, generosity, offerings, charity, and sacrifice. Christians give because they serve a giving God—the giver of every good gift, the source of life and love.

Jesus' teachings abound with tales of rich and poor, generous and shrewd, givers and takers, charitable and selfish, faithful and fearful. He commends the poor widow putting her two coins in the treasury; giving out of her poverty, she "put in all she had to live on" (Luke 21:1-4). The story upsets expectations by pointing to proportion rather than amount as the measure of extravagance.

Jesus' unexpected love for Zacchaeus so radically changes the tax collector that he gives his wealth to the poor and to those whom he has wronged. Giving serves justice and is a fruit of Christ's transforming grace (Luke 19:1-10).

The story of the good Samaritan highlights extraordinary generosity. The Samaritan not only binds up the wounds of the stranger left to die in the road, but he takes the stranger to an inn, pays for the stranger's care, and commits himself to provide for the long-term well-being of the stranger (Luke 10:35). The Samaritan's generosity, like Christ's compassion, knows no bounds.

And beyond all the teachings and parables, the followers of Jesus see in the gracious and costly gift of his sacrifice and death the ultimate self-revelation of God. The most memorized Scripture of the New Testament expresses the infinite nature of God's gracious love revealed in the gift we have received in Christ: "For God so loved the world that he gave his only Son" (John 3:16).

In these Scriptures above—the widow giving all she had, Zacchaeus in his transformation, the Samaritan with his compassion, and God's self-giving in Christ—giving is always *extravagant*, life changing, and joyous.

God uses our practice of giving to reconfigure our interior life. By giving, we craft a different inner desire as the driving element of life. Our motivations change.

People give because generosity helps them achieve God's purposes in *themselves*. By giving, we develop the inner qualities of generosity. Generosity is not a spiritual attribute someone acquires apart from the practice of giving. It becomes discernable only through visible behavior. We cannot become generous and hold on to everything we have for ourselves without letting go. The opposite of generosity is greediness, selfishness. These are not the qualities that lead to life, and so by our giving we cultivate a different nature inside ourselves.

- How does God use your giving to change you?
- Have you ever experienced a time when you felt led by God to increase your giving?

ALIGNED WITH GOD'S PURPOSES

> *"They . . . gave according to their means, and even*
> *beyond their means, begging us earnestly for the*
> *privilege of sharing in this ministry to the saints."*
> *— 2 Corinthians 8:3-4*

In his letter to the Corinthians, Paul commends the generosity of communities of faith, especially those who remain surprisingly extravagant in their giving during difficult travails. Writing of the churches of Macedonia, he says "for during a severe ordeal of affliction, their abundant joy and their extreme poverty have overflowed in a wealth of generosity on their part" (2 Corinthians 8:2). The notion that stewardship rightly focuses on the Christian's need to give rather than the church's need to receive is a spiritually powerful truth. The practice of tithing blesses and benefits the giver as much as it strengthens the mission and ministry of the church.

Still we wonder, does our giving really make a difference? What does our generosity have to do with our spiritual lives?

One reason many people give is simply because they love their church and they want the life-changing ministries of their congregation to prosper. They are themselves the beneficiaries of the church's ministries and they do their share to pay for the bills, the salaries, the facilities, and the costs so that the church can offer outreach, children's ministries, worship, and mission. They support the church so that others can receive what they have received. The fruit of this giving is tangible and visible; it is both immediate and long-term. Churches with generous members offer more ministry, work with greater confidence, have less conflict, and make a greater impact on their communities and on the world. Responsibility and hope for the church motivate the giver. People want their congregations to thrive.

People also give because their contribution aligns with the purposes God wants them to fulfill in the world. Helping people, relieving suffering, teaching the spiritual life, reaching young people—when we sense God's call to make a difference, we can contribute our time or become personally involved in the day-to-day ministry. Another way to make a difference is through giving, contributing the resources that make possible the work that we feel called to support. We please God by making the difference God wants us to make.

- How does God use your generosity to help your congregation to thrive?
- What's the largest gift you have ever given? What motivated you? What resulted from the gift? How were you affected?

HOW MUCH DO WE NEED?

*"Take care! Be on your guard against all kinds of greed; for one's life does not consist in the abundance of possessions." — **Luke 12:15***

Tolstoy, in "How Much Land Does a Man Need?" writes about a man, Pakhom, who farms the land given to him by his father. He wants more, so he saves and sacrifices until he expands his acreage, and even this is not enough. He hears about another region where more land can be bought with less money, so he sells his farm and moves his family across the country to the larger spread. Still, he is dissatisfied. Finally, he hears about a place where the king is offering an extraordinary deal. If you give the king all your money, you may take possession of all the land you can personally encompass by walking around it in a single day. Pakhom imagines how far he could walk in a day, and all the land he could own. He sells all his property and pays the king in exchange for his chance to walk the perimeters of the land that will be his.

A stake is hammered into the ground before sunrise. Pakhom must return to the stake before sunset, and all the land that he circles before that time will be his. As the day dawns, he runs at full speed in order to cover as much territory as possible. As the day heats up, he slows down and begins to circle back, but he sees lush pastures that he must possess, so he extends his path to include them. As the sun moves lower, he realizes that he has miscalculated, and he fears that he may not return to his starting place in time. He runs harder to reach the stake before sunset, pushing himself beyond exhaustion. He comes within view of his destination with only minutes to go. Pushing dangerously beyond his body's capacity to continue, he collapses and dies within reach of the stake.

How much land does a person need? Tolstoy ends his short story by saying that "six feet from head to heel" was all he needed.[3] Why are we discontent with what we have?

Giving puts us in a healthier relationship with our possessions, and with the material world in which we live. We like making money, but we enjoy other things as well, such as the love of our family; belonging to community; a sense of meaning, accomplishment, contribution, and service. We enjoy making a positive difference in the lives of other people. But how do we maintain balance and perspective? How can we appropriately secure the basic needs of food, shelter, education, and health while also living with purpose? How do we avoid too much preoccupation with the things that do not ultimately satisfy, and cultivate those things that do? The intentional practice of generosity helps us keep our priorities straight.

Giving reflects the nature of God. We give because we are made in the image of God, whose essential nature is giving. We are created with God's nature imprinted on our souls; we are hard-wired to be social, compassionate, connected, loving, and generous. God's extravagant generosity is part of our essential nature as well. But we are anxious and fearful, influenced by a culture that makes us believe we never have enough. God sent Jesus Christ to bring us back to ourselves, and back to God. As we *"have in us the mind that was in Christ Jesus,"* we become free.

Growing in the grace of giving is part of the Christian journey of faith, a response Christian disciples offer to God's call to make a difference in the world. Generosity enlarges the soul, realigns priorities, connects people to the body of Christ, and strengthens congregations to fulfill Christ's ministries.

- Do you sometimes feel that your life consists in the abundance of your possessions?
- How can practicing generosity counteract greed and begin to balance the priorities of your life?

Thursday

I HAVE LEARNED TO BE CONTENT

*"I have learned to be content with whatever I have. I know what it is to have little, and I know what it is to have plenty. . . . I can do all things through him who strengthens me." — **Philippians 4:11-13***

Generosity derives from a profound reorientation in our thinking about how we find contentment in life. Paul writes, "I have learned to be content with whatever I have," but Paul was not a slacker, lacking in initiative! He was industrious, competitive, and ambitious for the work of God. Paul realized how seductive our activity and our appetite for more could become. We begin to believe that happiness depends upon outward circumstance and material comforts rather than deriving from inner spiritual qualities—love, peace, compassion, self-control, gentleness, prayerfulness. Possessing greater wealth does not mean that we experience contentedness. We can still feel panic, emptiness, striving, and isolation. We feel needy, and our appetites become insatiable. Surrounded by water, we are dying of thirst.

Breaking the cycle of conditioned discontent requires courageous soul work. Abundant living derives from generative relationships, from mutual support, and from knowing how

58

to love and be loved. Contentment arises from seeking that which satisfies.

Contentedness comes from personal integrity, a life aligned with high values, depth of spirit and of mind, growth in grace and peace. These grant release from agitation, from unhealthy striving, and from continual dissatisfaction. Founded on these, we may value many of the things our culture induces us to seek, but without the harmful, destructive intensity. We want to improve our conditions and standing, but we don't embrace these objectives with the panicked intensity our society would have us do.

Primarily, contentedness is formed in us by the practice of generosity. Contentedness is learning to be happy with what we have rather than feeling distressed by what we lack. In our voluntarily giving away part of our wealth and earnings, we are saying, "I can spend all of this on myself, but I choose not to." In that simple act, repeated and deepened with frequency and intentionality, we break the bonds of self-destructive acquisitiveness.

Second, contentedness results from a deep, cultivated sense of gratitude. Generous people are thankful. They give thanks in all things, and their gratefulness sharpens their awareness of the deeper sources of happiness and from the spiritual awareness that God has already provided us everything we need to flourish. All is grace upon grace.

Finally, contentedness comes from persistent interior work and cooperation with the Holy Spirit to develop the personal habits that keep us from surrendering our sense of well-being, identity, and purpose to materialist measures. Living fruitfully is not merely a matter of having something to live on, but something to live for. Purpose, connection, love, service, friendship, family, generosity—these sustain contentedness.

- What causes you to feel content? How do you avoid a self-destructive acquisitiveness?
- What personal habits help to keep you grounded in Christ?

Friday

THE GOD-RELATED LIFE

*"It is easier for a camel to go through the eye of a needle than for a rich man to enter the kingdom of God." — **Mark 10:25, NIV***

We cannot "pay" our way to a closer relationship with God; whether giving aids us in our relationship with God or not depends upon our inner attitude. However, an unrestrained appetite for wealth or clinging too tightly to what we possess can hold us back and cause us paralysis in our following of Christ.

Scripture reminds us that "the love of money is a root of all kinds of evil" (1 Timothy 6:10), and "it is easier for a camel to go through the eye of a needle than for a rich man to enter the kingdom of God" (Mark 10:25, NIV). The rich young ruler cannot relinquish his wealth and so he forfeits life with Christ (Luke 18:18-25), the farmer builds bigger barns to store his possessions while avoiding eternal priorities and he loses his soul (12:16-21), the wealthy person ignores the sufferings of Lazarus at his doorstep and finds himself separated from God (16:19-31), the servant buries his talents instead of using them for his master and receives condemnation (19:12-26), and Ananias and Sapphira perish for their deceit that was motivated by their desire to keep their money (Acts 5:1-10).

Our clinging and coveting and hungering for wealth can obstruct our pathway to God and to the life God would have us enjoy. When unrestrained desire for material riches occupies the soul, there is little room left for God. Like Paul's assistant, Demas, we fall too much "in love with this present world," and we abandon Jesus' mission (2 Timothy 4:10). Greed impedes growth in Christ.

On the other hand, by giving generously, our beliefs and trust in God rise to tangible form. We become doers of the word and not hearers only. Giving makes following God real. We can live a God-related life or we can live without attention to God's presence and will. The God-related life means our relationship with God influences all we do. When we seek to do the things God would have us do, including giving, our practice intensifies our love for the things God loves. Then the material possessions that can serve as a distraction or impediment to following Christ become an instrument for our serving Christ. Our material goods, consecrated to God, nourish our desire to serve God. Generosity feeds our love for God.

- How does the practice of generosity affect your relationship with God?
- In terms of wealth and generosity, what does living a "God-related life" mean to you?

Tithing Is a Life Choice

"Test me in this and see if I don't open up heaven itself to you and pour out blessings beyond your wildest dreams." — ***Malachi 3:10,*** **The Message**

The practice of tithing provides a concrete way for us to take the words we speak, "God is Lord of my life," and put them into practice. Our commitment becomes tangible; our giving becomes a way of putting God first, an outward sign of an inner spiritual alignment.

Tithing provides a consistent and universal baseline, a theologically and biblically faithful standard, that is nominal enough to allow people of nearly any income to meet without imposing great hardship and yet large enough to stretch us and to cause us to do the necessary reordering of our priorities that spiritually reconfigures our values.

Tithing challenges us to ask ourselves, Is my giving generous? Or merely expedient? Do I give for practical reasons to help the church, or for spiritual reasons to nourish my spirit?

The practice of tithing is not merely about what God wants us to do, but about the kind of person God wants us to become. Does the giving I now practice help me develop a Christ-like heart?

Tithing alone is not sufficient to fully meet what the gift and demand of God's grace requires of Jesus' followers. The voices of the prophets ring the warning that people cannot expect material sacrifices alone to please God but that God's reign requires justice, righteousness, and faithfulness (Amos 5:21-24; Micah 6:8). People of God are to practice justice and compassion without neglecting the tithe (Matthew 23:23-24).

Tithing requires honest prayer. What would God have me do? Are there things God would want me to give up in order to tithe? The practice causes us to adapt our behaviors to someone else's will: God's. No one tithes accidentally. Extravagant Generosity requires focused soul work, deep conviction, a mature spirit, learning, practice, and extraordinary intentionality. Tithing is not merely a financial decision; it is a life choice that rearranges all the furniture of our interior lives. That's why we do it. Tithing blesses us.

- Have you practiced the tithe, regularly offering ten percent of income to God? If not, what keeps you from doing so? Do you desire to do so? How do you think it would affect your spiritual life?

PRACTICING GENEROSITY

*"You will be enriched in every way for your great
generosity." — 2 Corinthians 9:11*

The practice of Extravagant Generosity stretches us to offer our utmost and highest to God rather than to give in a manner that is haphazard, unplanned, reactive, minimalist, mediocre, or mechanical. *Extravagant* does not correspond with giving that is merely dutiful, required, burdensome, mandated, or simply doing one's part. *Extravagant* denotes a style and attitude of giving that is unexpectedly joyous, without predetermined limits, from the heart.

People who practice Extravagant Generosity change their lives in order to become more generous. They become rich in giving. They do not wait to be asked. When they see a need, they step forward to meet it, offering their resources as a means of help. They look at difficult financial times through the eyes of faith rather than of fear. They persist in doing good. They give in all seasons.

They enjoy giving. They pray and hope and dream about the good they accomplish through their gifts. They consecrate their giving to God. They delight in generosity. They give expecting nothing in return.

People who practice Extravagant Generosity learn to enjoy things without possessing them, to moderate their acquisitiveness, and to find satisfaction in simpler things. They avoid personal debt as much as possible. They save. They avoid overindulgence and waste. Their possessions do not rule them. They aspire, like Paul, to know the secret of being content with what they have. They give thanks in all circumstances. Love is a gift, and life is grace.

People who practice Extravagant Generosity change lives. Their giving knows no bounds. They are rich toward God.

- What obstacles prevent you from giving extravagantly? How would the practice of greater generosity change you?
- When was a time you felt God's Spirit move you to give resources beyond what you had previously practiced? How does your giving to God influence other aspects of your life?

Week Three Reflections

WEEK FOUR

THERE IS ALWAYS A WAY

*One poor widow came up and put in two small
coins. . . . Jesus . . . said, ". . . All the others gave what
they'll never miss; she gave extravagantly what she
couldn't afford—she gave her all."*
— *Mark 12:42-44,* **The Message**

For hundreds of generations, the practice of tithing has
sustained growth in personal generosity. To tithe means to give
a tenth, and involves returning to God ten percent of income.
It's simple, concise, and consistent. Write down your income
for the month, move the decimal point over one place, and
write a check to the church for the amount you see. Do it first
thing when you are paid, and you discover that the practice
dials down appetites, reshapes priorities, and that all other expenses, needs, and savings will readjust. What could be easier?

A friend told me that the first time he wrote a tithe check,
it felt like he'd swallowed an avocado pit! For most people,
tithing is not easy. It takes time to learn and adapt and grow
into the practice.

Some people perceive the tithe to be nothing more than a
left-over from an Old Testament law-based theology. They
think it is an arbitrary rule with little relevance today.

And yet Jesus commended the practice, even among the
Pharisees whom he criticized for making a show of their

self-righteousness. The early church practiced the tithe, and so have Christians in every generation since. John Wesley tithed and expected early Methodists to give regularly and generously at every class meeting and chapel service. Their gifts were meticulously recorded so that people could hold themselves accountable to the practice of giving.

The people whom we admire and respect for their generous spirits, spiritual wisdom, and deep-heartedness invariably have practiced giving in such an extravagant manner that it has reshaped them. God has used their long-term patterns of giving to form in them the spiritual qualities that cause them to be our mentors. They give extravagantly according to their means, and many beyond their means, and most practice or exceed the tithe.

Name one person you admire and respect because of all they *keep* for themselves. Name someone you consider generous and spiritually mature who constantly complains about giving, or who always seeks to give the least amount required. Largeness of spirit leads to an eagerness to give our utmost and highest.

Despite the outward challenges and inner struggles, and the countercultural nature of generosity, where there is a desire to give, there is a way. The two coins dropped in the treasury from the hands of the poor widow, noticed by Jesus and recorded for all time as a model of Extravagant Generosity, forever reminds us that there is always a way. Giving helps us become what God wants us to be.

- What kind of person do you want to become over the next ten years? What kind of person do you believe God desires you to become?
- How are your current practices of living taking you there? How is your generosity helping you become who God wants you to be?

TEACHING THE TITHE

"Make an offering of ten percent, a tithe, of all the produce which grows in your fields year after year. Bring this into the Presence of GOD, your God, at the place he designates for worship."
— *Deuteronomy 14:22*, The Message

Tithing helps the followers of Jesus understand that all things belong to God and that, during their days on earth, followers are entrusted as stewards to use all they have and all they are in ways that glorify God. What Christians *earn* belongs to God, and they should earn it honestly and in ways that serve purposes consistent with being followers of Christ. What Christians *spend* belongs to God, and they should use it wisely, not foolishly, on things that enhance life and do not diminish it. What they *save* belongs to God, and they should invest in ways that strengthen society. What Christians *give* belongs to God, and they need to give generously, extravagantly, and conscientiously in ways that strengthen the body of Christ and serve the mission of Christ.

One hundred and fifty years ago, if your great-grandparents were active in the faith, they tithed. Why were they able to tithe one hundred and fifty years ago, but yet we have trouble doing it today? Because they were so much wealthier than we are? The truth is precisely the opposite! We struggle with tithing because our hearts and minds are more powerfully shaped by our affluence. We find it harder to give extravagantly because our society's values shape our perceptions more than our faith's values do.

Those who are new to the faith may find the practice of tithing extremely challenging. Take it one step at a time and grow into it over a few years. If you are so overwhelmed with debt that you struggle under an oppressive anxiety, first make the changes in spending and lifestyle that grant you freedom from excessive debt. When you can breathe again, begin to give proportionally, and grow in the grace of giving toward the tithe.

On the other hand, those who have been active in the faith for twenty, thirty, or forty years and have attended worship faithfully and studied Scripture in classes and felt sustained by the fellowship of the church and offered themselves in service to others in Christ's name, but who do not tithe . . . I would simply challenge you to think seriously and prayerfully about why this is. Why are the other faith practices relevant and helpful, but the discipline of tithing is not? Is the avoidance of tithing a fruit of faithfulness, or the result of submission to the values of a consumerist culture?

Practice the tithe. Teach children to spend wisely, to save consistently, and to give generously. Let them learn from their parents and grandparents so that they will be generous and not greedy, giving and not self-indulgent, charitable and not self-absorbed. Extravagant Generosity changes the life and spirit of the giver.

- How did you first learn about tithing? Have you seen others practice the tithe? How does it shape their lives?
- Do you tithe? If so, why? If not, why not? What causes you to resist growing in generosity?
- How do you teach and model generosity for the next generation?

THROUGH GOD'S EYES

*"Don't become so well adjusted to your culture that you fit in without even thinking. Instead, fix your attention on God. You'll be changed from the inside out." — **Romans 12:1-2,** **The Message***

Vibrant, fruitful, growing congregations thrive because of the extraordinary sharing, willing sacrifice, and joyous giving of their members out of love for God and neighbor. Such churches teach and practice giving that focuses on the abundance of God's grace and that emphasizes the Christian's need to give rather than on the church's need for money. In the spirit and manner of Christ, congregations that practice Extravagant Generosity explicitly talk about the place of money in the Christian's walk of faith. They view giving as a gift from God and are driven to be generous by a high sense of mission and a keen desire to please God by making a positive difference in the world.

The notion that giving rightly focuses on our need to give rather than on the church's need to receive is not a money-raising strategy, but a spiritually powerful truth. The practice of tithing benefits the giver as much as it strengthens the mission and ministry of the church.

Americans live in an extraordinarily materialist and consumerist society. We are immersed in a culture that feeds acquisitiveness, the appetite for more and bigger, and that fosters the myth that self-worth is found in material wealth and that happiness comes by possessing. Thirty-year-olds feel like failures because they don't already have the kind of house that their parents own. Couples struggle under oppressive levels of debt that strain marriages, destroy happiness, and intensify conflict and anxiety. As one radio show host says, "We buy things we don't even need with money we don't even have to impress people we don't even know!" (*The Dave Ramsey Show*).

At root, these are spiritual problems, not merely financial planning issues. They reveal belief systems that are spiritually corrosive and that lead to continuing discontent, discouragement, and unhappiness. We can never earn enough to be happy when we believe that satisfaction, self-definition, and meaning derive principally from our possessions, and we can never trust our sense of self-worth when it rests on treasures that are material and temporal. A philosophy based principally upon materialism, acquisition, and possessions is not sufficient to live by, or to die by. At some point, followers of Jesus must decide whether they will listen to the wisdom of the world or to the wisdom of God.

- How does living generously help you see the world through God's eyes?

- How is your own philosophy of life shaped by materialism, acquisition, and the desire to possess? How is it shaped by the wisdom of God? How do you resolve the tensions?

THE OLD LIFE AND THE NEW LIFE

> *"You're done with that old life. It's like a filthy set of*
> *ill-fitting clothes you've stripped off and put in the*
> *fire. . . . So, chosen by God for this new life of love,*
> *dress in a wardrobe God picked out for you: compas-*
> *sion, kindness, humility, quiet strength, discipline. . . .*
> *And regardless of what else you put on, wear love.*
> *It's your basic all-purpose garment. Never be without*
> *it."* — *Colossians 3:9, 12, 14,* **The Message**

Vines, branches, seedtime, harvest, soils, vineyards, trees, fruits—the Bible is replete with stories that lift high the notion that God expects us to use what we have received to make a positive difference in the world around us. Fruitfulness points us toward the result, the impact, and the outcome of our work for God's purposes and saves us from merely congratulating ourselves on our efforts, our hard work, or our input.

But as any gardener knows, the biblical stories of plants and seeds and growth and vines and branches are incomplete without the idea of pruning. Some things must go. Some min- istries are no longer fruitful and some programs have served their time and are no longer relevant or effective. Fruitfulness reminds us to ask ourselves, "Do our ministries really change lives and transform the world?"

Peter Drucker, the organizational expert who focused much of his professional energy on churches and non-profits in the later years of his career, offers this as one of his top lessons for church leaders: Practice *planned abandonment*. Planned abandonment involves intentionally closing down work that no longer contributes to the mission.

According to Drucker, the purpose of any non-profit organization is the changed life. If we are doing work and offering ministries that are no longer shaping lives in significant ways, perhaps we should stop doing them. As we initiate new ministries, create more effective mission projects, and plan how to better reach people, are there also services, activities, and outreach ministries that we need to reduce? How do we redirect our time, energy, and financial resources toward the ministries that most help us fulfill our mission? These are tough questions, but they are questions of stewardship. Jesus says, "Even now the ax is lying at the root of the trees; every tree therefore that does not bear good fruit is cut down and thrown into the fire" (Luke 3:9). If it's no longer bearing kingdom fruit, stop doing it.

Notions of fruitfulness and pruning also apply as we reflect on attitudes and behaviors in ourselves. In order for us to nurture the interior fruit of the Spirit—love, joy, peace, patience, kindness, generosity, faithfulness, gentleness, and self-control—we must leave behind enmity, anger, dissensions, and things like these (Galatians 5:19-23).

If we desire to become more generous, as I believe God would want for us, we will have to make some practical decisions that cause us to leave some behaviors behind. To give more to God may mean reprioritizing and spending less on other things that do not lend life and build us up. We may have to prune some expenses and change some spending habits to nurture greater generosity.

No one tithes accidentally. No one happens to have enough money left over at the end of the month to be truly generous. Extravagant Generosity requires intentionality. Tithing results from deep commitment, but also from carefully planning. We do it willingly, and willfully, or we never do it at all. We have to think about it, pray about it, talk it over, and plan for it. It's a major decision involving everyone in the household. It requires us to change, and to begin to seek God's priorities instead of merely our own.

The apostle Paul uses another image beside fruitfulness and pruning to describe the change that God works within us by the Holy Spirit when we follow Christ. He says that new life in Christ is like getting rid of old ill-fitting clothing and putting on new clothes that God has picked out for us (see above, from Colossians 3). Elsewhere Paul writes, "Everything . . . connected with that old way of life has to go. It's rotten through and through. Get rid of it! And then take on an entirely new way of life—a God-fashioned life, a life renewed from the inside and working itself into your conduct as God accurately reproduces his character in you" (Ephesians 4:23-24, *The Message*).

- What attitudes, behaviors, and values might you need to prune in order to live more fruitfully in Christ?
- How much planning, praying, and intentionality do you put into your decisions about giving? How would giving more generously require changes inside you and in your behaviors?

ONE OF MY OWN

*"This most generous God who gives seed to the
farmer that becomes bread for your meals is more
than extravagant with you. He gives you something
you can then give away, which grows into full-
formed lives, robust in God, wealthy in every way, so
that you can be generous in every way . . ."*
— 2 Corinthians 9:11, **The Message**

A long-time member and proud grandfather stood at the
baptismal font with his family for the baptism of his baby
granddaughter. Another infant from another family that was
new to the congregation was baptized at the same service. Following the service, the two families intermingled at the front
of the church as they took turns having their pictures taken. At
one point, the mother from the new family needed to get some
things out of her bag, and the grandfather from the other family offered to hold her baby. Other church members com-
mented on the grandfather with the baby; and he found himself
saying several times, "Oh, this one isn't mine; I'm just holding
him for a minute."

Monday morning the grandfather visited the pastor at the
church office and said, "I want to change my will to include the
church, and I want to talk to you about how to do that." The

pastor was stunned and couldn't help asking about what brought the grandfather to this decision. The older man's eyes grew moist as he said, "Yesterday I realized something while I was holding that other baby. I kept telling people that he wasn't my child, but then it dawned on me that he was part of my family, part of my church family. I've been a member of this church for more than forty years, and in God's eyes I'm a grandfather to more than just my own. I've taken care of my own children with my will, but I realized I also need to provide for the children of the church. So I want to divide my estate to leave a part to the church as if the church were one of my children."

Those who practice Extravagant Generosity have a God-given vision and faith to plant seeds for trees whose shade they will never see.

- How have those who have come before you in your family, community, and church paved an easier road for you through their generosity?
- How have you paved the road for those who will follow in the faith through your generosity?

Saturday

GENEROUS CONGREGATIONS

"What matters most to me is to finish what God started: the job the Master Jesus gave me of letting everyone I meet know all about this incredibly extravagant generosity of God." — Acts 20:24, **The Message**

Churches that cultivate Extravagant Generosity hold high quality annual pledge opportunities with wide participation, excellent preparation, and active lay involvement. While pastors provide leadership through preaching, teaching, and example, congregations rely heavily on the witness of extravagantly generous lay persons though testimonies, sermons, leadership talks, newsletter meditations, and website devotionals. They invite people into leadership who speak with integrity because of their own personal growth in the practice of giving, including people of diverse ages, incomes, and backgrounds.

Vibrant, fruitful, growing congregations focus on giving during the season of annual pledging, but they also emphasize generosity throughout the year in preaching, Bible studies, and classes. They speak about how our relationship with God affects our views of money and how our relationship with money shapes our relationship to God. They teach about the place of wealth, affluence, acquisitiveness, materialism, selfishness, generosity, and giving. They do not avoid capital funds campaigns when they serve the mission of the church, and they enter into major projects with excellence, professional preparation, and outstanding communication. They regularly offer members the opportunity to support special appeals and new projects, knowing that giving stimulates giving; and they've learned that when special giving is aligned with the purposes of Christ, it enhances support for the general budget rather than diminishes it. They readily encourage charitable contributions and philanthropic giving by their members to service agencies and to medical, advocacy, and cultural causes that make a difference in the lives of people.

Such churches do more than encourage, teach, and support *personal* generosity, they practice Extraordinary Generosity *as a congregation*, demonstrating exemplary support for special projects, missions in the community and around the world, and denominational connectional ministries. They take the lead in responding to disasters and unexpected emergencies. Pastors and lay leaders view "giving beyond the walls" as indispensable to Christian discipleship and to congregational mission and vitality. They look for more and better opportunities to make a positive difference in the lives of people. They develop mission partnerships; support agencies that help the poor; and fund mission teams, scholarships, service projects, new church starts, and other ministries that transform lives. They make the mission of the church real, tangible, and meaningful. Their reputation for generosity bears witness to Christ.

Churches that grow in giving know that generosity increases with participation in ministry and community, and so they work to deepen the core ministries of worship, small-group learning, and mission. Many churches do not have enough money because they don't provide sufficient ministry and mission. Rather than becoming obsessed with income, survival, and maintenance, generous congregations continually return their focus to changing lives, reaching new people, and offering significant mission. By growing in ministry, giving increases.

Congregations that practice Extravagant Generosity teach, model, and cultivate generosity among children and youth. Sunday school classes, after-school children's ministries, vacation Bible school, and youth ministries all offer opportunities to give individually and to work together in groups to achieve a ministry goal that is significant, tangible, and compelling. Rather than collecting offerings in a perfunctory way, children's and youth leaders explain, teach, and connect the action of giving to the work of God. Generous congregations equip parents with ideas, suggestions, and practices that foster generosity for children and youth of all ages.

- Would you describe your congregation as generous? Why? Why not?
- Would you describe yourself as generous? Extravagantly so?

DELIGHT

*"Tell those rich in this world's wealth to quit being
so full of themselves and so obsessed with money,
which is here today and gone tomorrow. Tell them to
go after God . . . to be rich in helping others, to be
extravagantly generous. If they do that, they'll build
a treasury that will last, gaining life that is truly
life."* — *1 Timothy 6:17-19,* **The Message**

People who practice Extravagant Generosity give with un-expected liberality, they make giving a first priority, and they plan their giving with great energy and passion. They go the second mile. They do not give from a "what remains" mentality, but from a "what comes first" priority. Giving seriously becomes a personal spiritual discipline, a way of serving God, and a means of helping the church fulfill its God-appointed mission. Focused conviction and intention causes them to give in a more pronounced way, without fear and with greater trust. Giving changes their lives.

Extravagant describes giving that is extraordinary, over-the-top, and propelled by great passion. *Extravagant* is the generosity seen in those who appreciate the beauty of giving, the awe and joy of making a difference for the purposes of Christ. Extravagant Generosity is giving to God as God has given to us.

People who practice Extravagant Generosity shift things around so that they can do more. Their generosity opens them to projects they never dreamed God would involve them in. They are conscientious and intentional. Generosity is their calling. They want to make a difference for Christ. They care.

They grow in the grace of giving. They learn. They take small steps until generosity becomes natural. They deepen their understanding of giving through prayer and Scripture, and they foster generosity in others. They give more now than in the past, and will give more in the future than they do today.

They push their congregations to become more generous. They advocate outward-focused ministry. They do not give in order to control the church but to support it. They excel in giving. They love to give. They are motivated by a desire to make a difference rather than by guilt, fear, desire for recognition, or to manipulate others. They give with humility. Yet, they draw others toward generosity and toward God through their example.

People who practice Extravagant Generosity teach their children and grandchildren to give, mentoring them on how to earn honestly, save carefully, spend prudently, and give lavishly.

They live with a sense of gratitude. They like receiving money, find pleasure in its responsible use, and experience joy in giving it to God's purposes. They do not become too attached, and are not stopped, deceived, slowed, misled, or detoured in their following of Christ by the possession of money. They delight in Jesus' way, the way of true life.

- How do you delight in the good you do through your giving?
- Do you give more now than in the past, and do you expect to give more in the future than you do today? How are you *learning* to give?

Week Four Reflections

_____

_____

_____

_____

_____

_____

_____

_____

_____

_____

_____

_____

_____

_____

_____

_____

_____

_____

_____

_____

NOTES

Week Two

[1] Charles Frazier, *Cold Mountain* (Atlantic Monthly Press, 1997); pp. 231–232.

[2] Frazier; pp. 232, 234.

Week Three

[3] Leo Tolstoy, *How Much Land Does a Man Need? and Other Stories* (Penguin, 1993); p. 110.